Fossil Fuels

Editor: John Clark
Editorial Planning: Clark Robinson Ltd
Design: David West
                     Children's Book Design
Illustrator: Aziz Khan
Picture research: Cecilia Weston-Baker
Photographic Credits:
Cover and pages 4-5, 6 both, 8, 11 both, 13, 17, 18, 20, 22, 29 top left and 29
bottom: J. Allan Cash Library; page 10: National Coal Board; pages 14 and
27 bottom left: Robert Harding Library; page 15: Bruce Coleman Ltd; page
19: Esso; page 21: Zefa Picture Libary; page 24: Shell; page 27 bottom right:
Yamaha; page 28: Spectrum Colour Library.

Created and designed by
Aladdin Books Ltd
28 Percy Street
London W1P 9FF

First published in
Great Britain in 1990 by
Gloucester Press
96 Leonard Street
London EC2A 4RH

ISBN 0-7496-0367-4

Printed in Belgium

The publishers would like to acknowledge that the photographs reproduced
within this book have been posed by models or have been obtained from
photographic agencies.

A CIP catalogue record for this book is available from the British Library

Facts on

Fossil Fuels

Clint Twist

GLOUCESTER PRESS
London · New York · Toronto · Sydney

CONTENTS

INTRODUCTION

Fossil fuels are the Earth's most valuable source of energy. This energy originally came from the Sun, was transformed into the living bodies of plants and animals, and has been stored for millions of years beneath the ground.

Electricity from coal lights our homes, gas cooks our meals, and oil provides petrol for cars, as well as many other useful substances. The development of modern civilization has been made possible by these three fossil fuels.

But fossil fuels are non-renewable resources. When we have used them all up, there will be no more. The exploitation of fossil fuels has made us accustomed to abundant and fairly cheap energy. The world must now start to use these resources more wisely, before it is too late.

◁ The Wahan steelworks, China

SEARCH FOR FUEL

Coal, oil and gas are among the Earth's hidden treasures, usually occurring many hundreds of metres underground, or under the sea bed. Deposits rarely betray their presence at the surface. Most of the world's coal was created during one period of geological time. By studying rock formations, geologists can usually predict fairly accurately where coal will be found. Oil and gas, however, are more difficult to find. Some deposits are very ancient while others are of relatively recent origin, and they occur in many rock types. Finding the deposits is made more difficult by the fact that oil and gas can flow through certain types of rock. Oil prospectors use many techniques in their search for oil. But the only real proof that a deposit of oil exists under a certain piece of the Earth's surface is to drill into the ground to find it.

Through a combination of experience and theory, geologists know that gas and oil deposits are often found in certain types of rock formation. The commonest is an anticline, a large dome-shaped structure that may not be apparent at the surface.

Offshore exploratory well

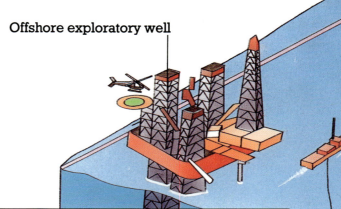

FOSSIL FUELS

Fossil fuels are the remains of past life that can be burned to provide heat. To survey for fossil fuels extensive use is made of satellite pictures (as in picture of the Himalayas left). For confirmation of the find it may well be necessary to use a test drilling (see picture below).

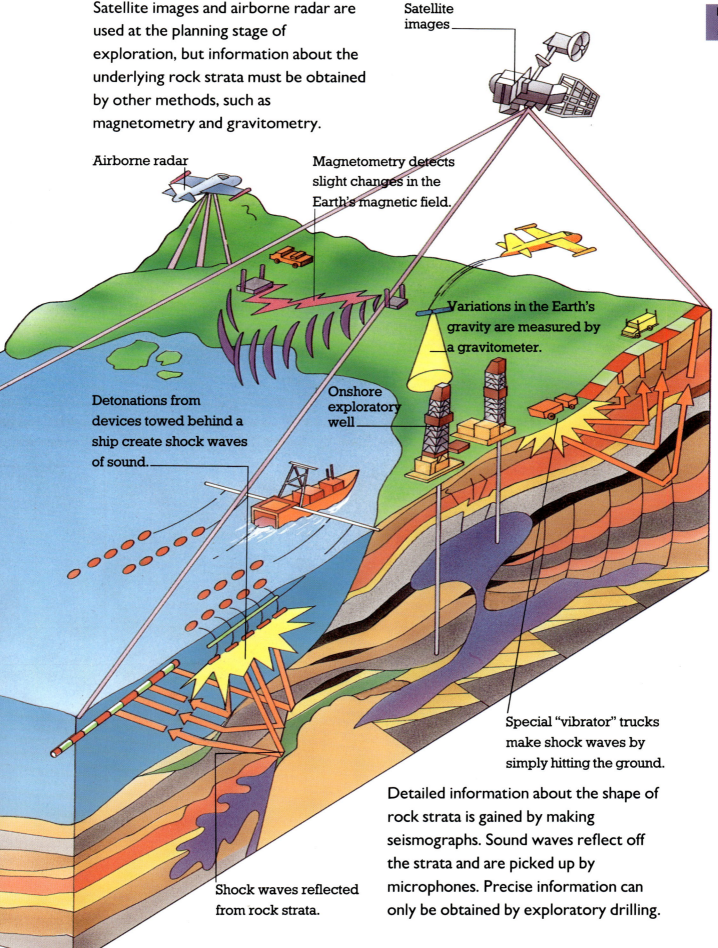

Satellite images and airborne radar are used at the planning stage of exploration, but information about the underlying rock strata must be obtained by other methods, such as magnetometry and gravitometry.

Satellite images

Airborne radar

Magnetometry detects slight changes in the Earth's magnetic field.

Variations in the Earth's gravity are measured by a gravitometer.

Detonations from devices towed behind a ship create shock waves of sound.

Onshore exploratory well

Special "vibrator" trucks make shock waves by simply hitting the ground.

Shock waves reflected from rock strata.

Detailed information about the shape of rock strata is gained by making seismographs. Sound waves reflect off the strata and are picked up by microphones. Precise information can only be obtained by exploratory drilling.

WHAT IS COAL?

Coal is the fossilized remains of plants, such as ferns and trees, that lived on Earth about 250 million years ago. It resembles black rock in appearance. Some types of coal are very hard and can be cut and polished like gemstones, while other types can be crumbled between the fingers. Coal burns because it contains the element carbon. The best quality coal consists of about 98 per cent carbon, with very few impurities. Average quality coal is only 70-85 per cent carbon, and the remaining 15-30 per cent is mainly water. Coal that has less than 60 per cent carbon content is no longer black and is known as brown coal or lignite. As well as the carbon and water, coal also contains varying amounts of methane gas and a thick liquid known as coal tar.

FORMATION

About 250 million years ago, large areas of the Earth were covered with swampy forests. As dead vegetation fell into the swamps, the forests gradually produced a thick layer of organic matter. Because the waterlogged conditions inhibited decay, this matter became preserved, first of all as a spongy brown substance known as peat. Sometimes, this was drowned beneath seas or lakes, and layers of sedimentary rock were laid down on top. The peat was slowly compressed into lignite and coal.

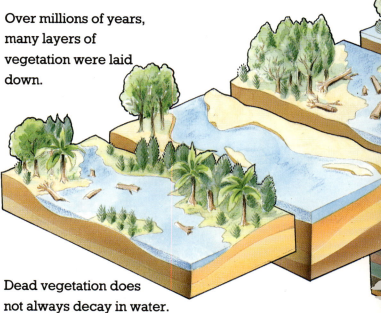

Over millions of years, many layers of vegetation were laid down.

Dead vegetation does not always decay in water.

DIFFERENT TYPES

When dry, peat can be burned, but little heat is given off. Lignite produces more heat, but it is difficult to handle. Cannel is a soft black coal.

Bituminous coal contains the highest quantity of coal tar, and is the most widely used. Anthracite contains at least 90 per cent carbon, and is the most expensive.

Peat

Cannel

Anthracite

Lignite

Bituminous coal

Coal occurs in bands known as seams. The rocks in which coal seams are found are known as coal measures.

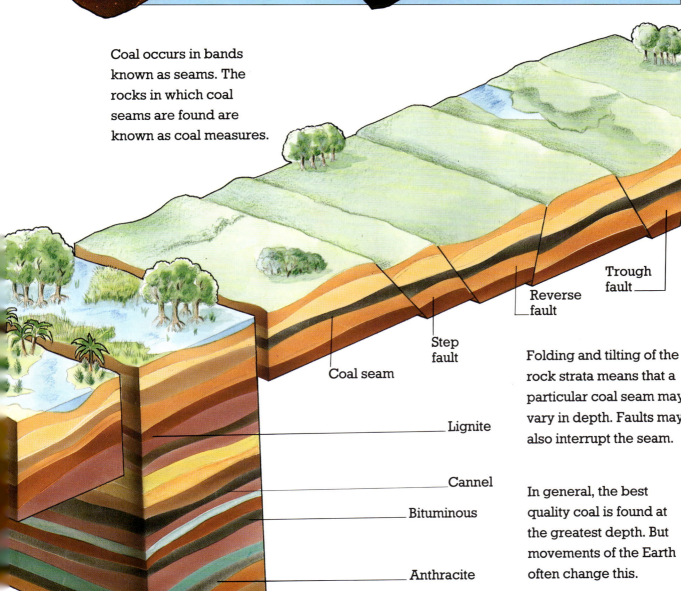

Trough fault

Reverse fault

Step fault

Coal seam

Lignite

Cannel

Bituminous

Anthracite

Folding and tilting of the rock strata means that a particular coal seam may vary in depth. Faults may also interrupt the seam.

In general, the best quality coal is found at the greatest depth. But movements of the Earth often change this.

COAL MINING

Coal deposits vary in location as well as in quality. A particular seam may be exposed to the surface at one location, yet be 3,000m underground a few kilometres away. Seams also differ greatly in thickness. In China, some seams are more than 100m thick; while in Britain, seams as narrow as 30cm are worked. When seams occur near the surface, the coal can be extracted by open-cast mining. The best quality coal, however, is usually obtained by deep mining, in which a vertical shaft is dug down to the coal seam. Horizontal tunnels or galleries are then cut into the seam as the coal is extracted. The deepest mines have galleries over 1,200m below ground. The introduction of modern machinery and equipment has greatly increased the efficiency of all types of coal mining.

THE LONG WALL

Taking coal from the sides of a tunnel is far more efficient than working just at the end. The long wall method enables a coal-face 100m long to be worked by machinery. The roof immediately in front of the coal-face is held up by immensely strong hydraulic supports. As mining advances, the supports are moved forward, and the area behind collapses. Other methods leave pillars of coal to support the roof.

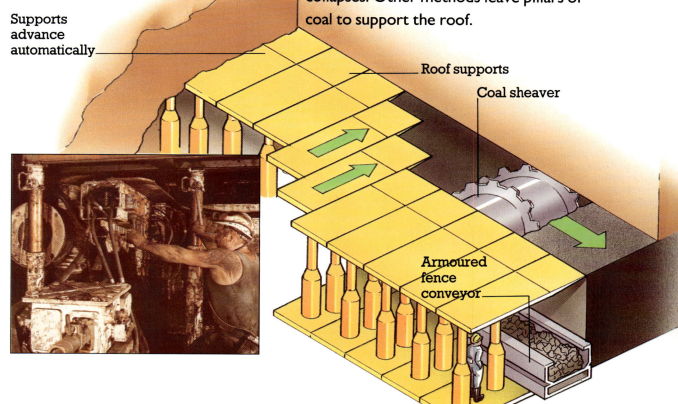

Supports advance automatically

Roof supports

Coal sheaver

Armoured fence conveyor

STRIP MINING

Conventional open-cast mining (digging a very large hole) can be very destructive to the landscape, especially when the coal underneath is valuable farmland. Strip mining ensures that the damage is only temporary.

Once strip mining has begun, the unwanted rock and soil (the overburden) is used to fill in previous excavations. The overburden may be up to 65m thick, and mining equipment includes huge shovels that can remove 100 cubic metres of earth in one bite.

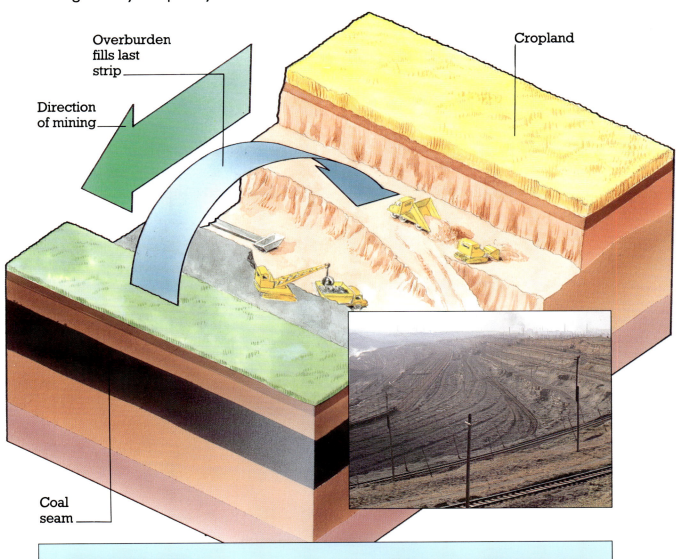

Overburden fills last strip

Direction of mining

Cropland

Coal seam

COAL SPOIL

All coal mining produces some non-flammable material (spoil), which has to be sorted out of the coal at the surface. This is usually dumped in huge, unsightly mounds, although nowadays, the mounds are often planted with grass and trees.

BURNING COAL

The use of coal as a fuel began at least 3,000 years ago, but it was used very little until the eighteenth century when supplies of firewood and charcoal began to run out. Demand for coal was further increased by the discovery of how to use a form of coal (coke) in iron-making and in gas manufacture. The Industrial Revolution made coal the most important industrial fuel in the world, and it became widely available as a domestic fuel in the fast-growing towns and cities. During the twentieth century, the use of oil and other fuels has reduced our dependence on coal. Huge quantities are still burned to generate electric power. But problems with air pollution that were caused by coal fires in people's houses has made it less popular as a domestic fuel in built-up areas.

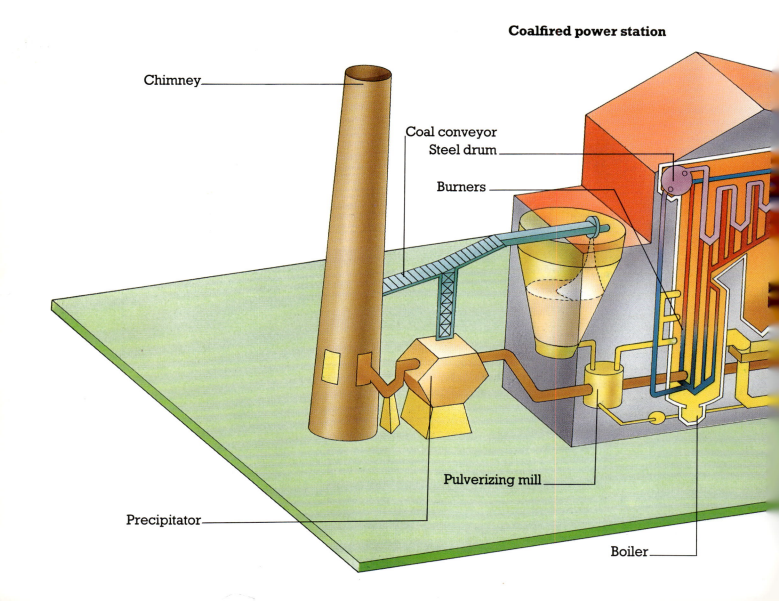

Coalfired power station

Chimney

Coal conveyor
Steel drum
Burners

Pulverizing mill

Precipitator

Boiler

Coal is a bulky and dirty material, and the energy it contains can be best used if it is first converted into electricity. Coal burns most efficiently when it has been crushed into fine particles, and most power stations have a pulverizing mill. Fans are used to blast a mixture of air and coal dust into the furnace beneath the boiler. Steam is piped from the boiler to the turbine. The turbine drives the generator. Once the steam has passed through the turbine, it is led away to cool in large towers. Most power stations now have precipitators which use static electricity to remove pollution-forming particles from the smoke and fumes given off by the burning coal. Others have installed equipment to remove sulphur dioxide.

STEELWORKS

Heating coke and iron ore together produces the raw material for steel-making. Coke is a form of almost pure carbon that is produced by baking bituminous coal.

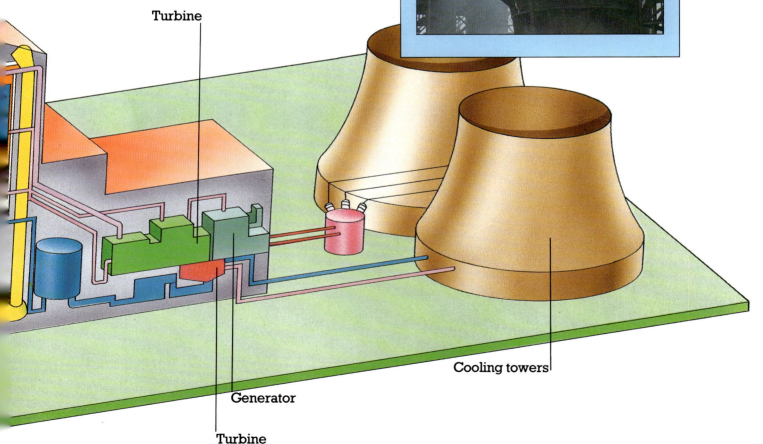

Turbine

Generator

Turbine

Cooling towers

OIL AND GAS

Crude oil that has come straight out of the ground is an extremely complex liquid that contains thousands of different chemical compounds. Nearly all of these compounds contain the elements carbon and hydrogen, and are known as hydrocarbons. At room temperature, some are gases, most are liquids, and a few are almost solid. Natural gas is methane – the same gas as is found in some types of coal. Although it sometimes occurs on its own as "dry" gas (almost pure methane), natural gas is usually found together with oil and contains many other hydrocarbons. Both oil and gas are found in porous rocks that hold them like a sponge holds water. Such areas of rock are known as reservoirs. A group of reservoirs is called a field.

OIL SHALES AND TAR SANDS

Oil does not always occur as a convenient liquid. In certain circumstances, oil can become spread through sand or shale (a type of layered rock) and form a semi-solid substance. It is estimated that two-thirds of the world's oil may exist in this form. Until recently it was too expensive to extract such oil. But as the oil that is easier to extract is being used up, the importance of other oil is increasing.

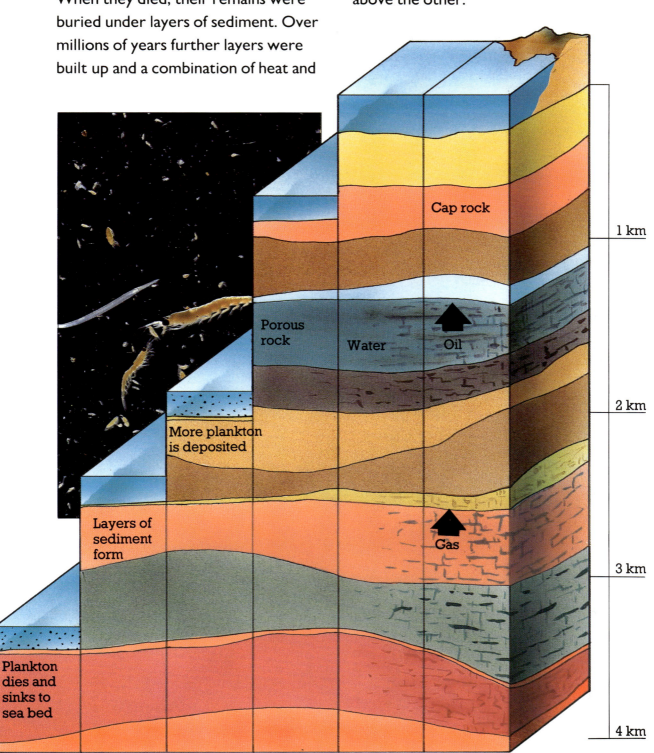

HOW THEY ARE MADE

Scientists believe that oil and most natural gas were produced from the bodies of minute sea creatures known as plankton. At various times in the past, the Earth's oceans contained much greater numbers of plankton than today. When they died, their remains were buried under layers of sediment. Over millions of years further layers were built up and a combination of heat and pressure produced oil and gas.

Gas and oil can move through certain types of rock, and tend to rise until they are trapped by a layer of "cap" rock. Oil floats on top of water, and gas rises above both. When the three are together, they are found separated one above the other.

Cap rock

Porous rock

Water

Oil

More plankton is deposited

Layers of sediment form

Gas

Plankton dies and sinks to sea bed

1 km

2 km

3 km

4 km

EXPLORATION

Even the best surveys can only show that oil might be under the ground. It is only possible to be certain it is there by drilling. Drilling a series of test holes (often to depths of over 6,000m) is a very expensive business. If the holes have to be drilled into rock that is underwater, the cost is multiplied many times. Drilling extracts rock samples from far beneath the surface and allows geologists to make a study of what lies underground. The samples are put through a variety of tests that show even the slightest trace of oil. The results are carefully studied. Only rarely does exploration drilling produce a free-flowing "gusher" of oil. Once oil has been shown to be present, exploration drilling is used for mapping the extent of the reservoir, and estimating its likely output.

DRILLING FOR OIL

Drilling provides a constant flow of information in the form of rock fragments brought to the surface by the "mud" used to lubricate the drill. When a precise picture is required, a special drill is used to cut a solid core of rock for examination. Oil prospectors have learned never to be surprised when drilling. Two holes drilled only a hundred metres apart can produce very different results, even on a known field.

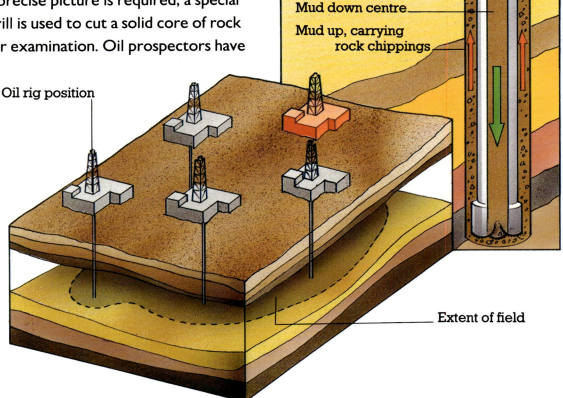

Oil rig position

Mud down centre

Mud up, carrying rock chippings

Extent of field

OFFSHORE RIGS

The search for offshore oil means coping with the additional problem of drilling under water. The first offshore oil-rigs were built like piers straight out from the coast, but were confined to very shallow water. For water up to 60m deep, modern rigs have jack-up legs that can be lowered after the rig has been floated into position. For deep water drilling (up to 1,000m), drill ships can be used. These are anchored firmly in position, but waves can make drilling very difficult. A semi-submersible rig is more stable. The rig is towed into position. Then the lower portion is flooded so that it sinks about 30m below the surface. At this depth, the waves have little effect, and the rig forms a stable platform suitable for drilling in water up to 600m deep.

EXPLORATION RIG

This test drilling rig is moving itself into position. The most distinctive feature is the derrick of scaffolding that supports the drill.

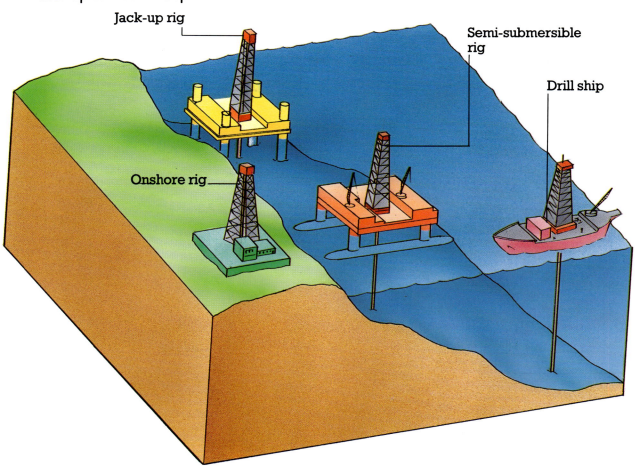

Jack-up rig

Semi-submersible rig

Drill ship

Onshore rig

PRODUCTION

Exploration can determine the extent of a field, and the exact nature of its contents. But a hole in the ground only becomes a well when it starts producing oil. Drilling a production well is a very skilled business. The best place to drill the well must be chosen. If oil and gas occur together, the gas will always be nearer the surface. In order to get a constant flow of oil, the well may have to be drilled at the edge of the field where there is no gas above the oil. Often, the pressure of the gas is used to force the oil up the well. When a well dries up, it does not always mean that there is no oil left. A deeper well may be drilled to reach the remaining oil, or water may be pumped into the reservoir in order to force the oil nearer to the surface so it can be extracted by the existing well.

DIRECTIONAL DRILLING

The recent development of directional drilling techniques enables a well to be drilled around any difficult areas of rock. Directional drilling is also extremely useful offshore, where moving a drilling rig can be a long and expensive task.

Wedge-shaped blocks, known as whipstocks, are fitted behind an angled bit to force the drill to cut in a particular direction. The position of the drill is monitored by electronic instruments.

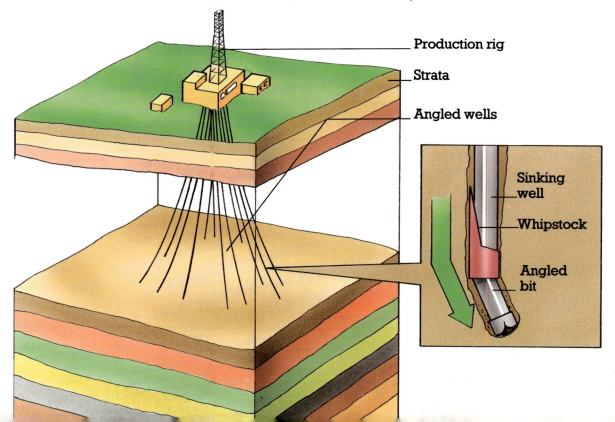

Production rig

Strata

Angled wells

Sinking well

Whipstock

Angled bit

WELL HEAD

If the oil or gas in the reservoir is under pressure, the flow out of the well must be regulated. At the well head, a system of valves, known as a "Christmas tree", diverts the flow into pipes as required.

At sea, the flow from several wells may be piped to a single production platform. On the platform, a series of Christmas trees controls the output to offshore terminals, or through underwater pipelines to the shore.

NODDING DONKEYS

In many parts of the world, oil has to be pumped to the surface. Often the only sign of the oilfield beneath the ground is the motion of the "nodding donkey" pumps. Some bring oil from more than 4km underground, and have been working non-stop for years.

TRANSPORTATION

Oil that has not yet been refined is known as crude oil. Crude oil is a liquid that is fairly safe and easy to handle. At normal temperatures, it can be pumped along pipes and stored in thin-walled metal tanks. With varying degrees of difficulty, the different forms of gas can be liquefied, but must then be kept in refrigerated or strengthened containers. Most long-distance transportation of oil and gas is by sea, in specially constructed tankers. The largest supertankers carry up to 500,000 tonnes of crude oil at a time. Gas tankers are generally much smaller. Oil and gas are usually loaded and unloaded at terminals located on the coast. Some countries have built off-shore terminals on islands or floating platforms. This is because some tankers are too big to come into ports.

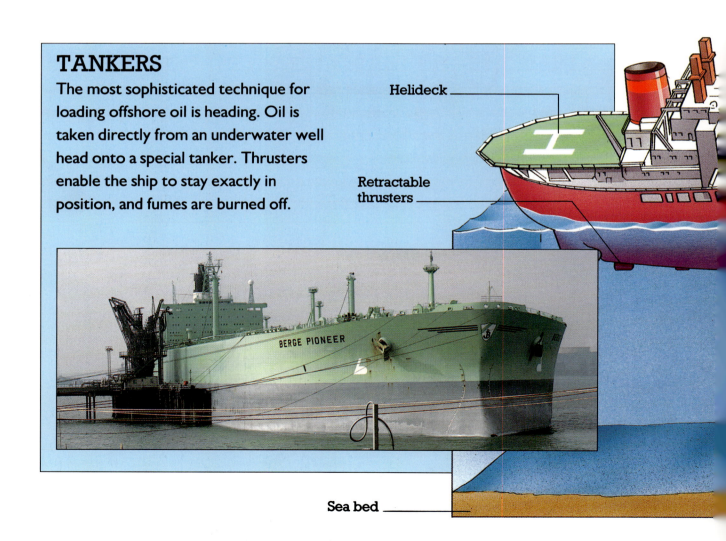

TANKERS
The most sophisticated technique for loading offshore oil is heading. Oil is taken directly from an underwater well head onto a special tanker. Thrusters enable the ship to stay exactly in position, and fumes are burned off.

Helideck

Retractable thrusters

BERGE PIONEER

Sea bed

PIPELINES

Pipelines are much more expensive than sea transport, and are mainly used for distribution over distances of not more than a few hundred kilometres. Plastic is now taking over from metal as a pipeline material, and pipe diameters vary from 20-200cm.

Exploitation of new fields in Alaska and Siberia, far enough north for the ocean to freeze in winter, has meant the construction of long overland pipelines. The Alaskan pipeline runs nearly 1,000km.

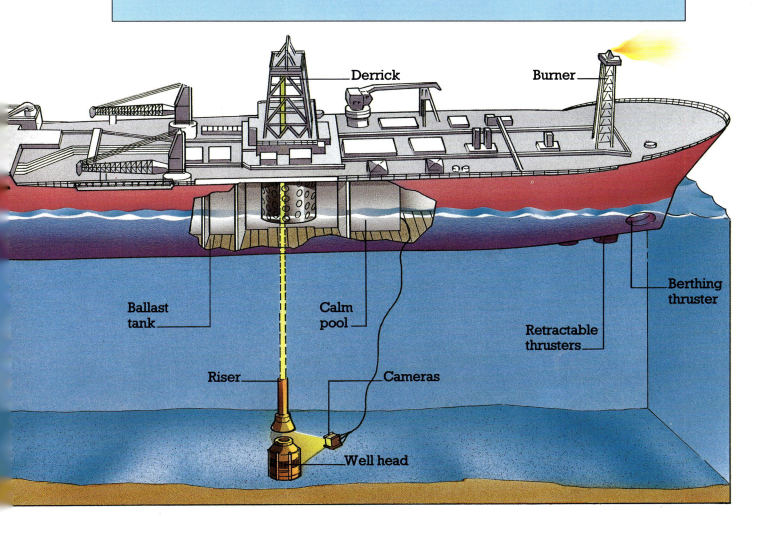

Derrick

Burner

Ballast tank

Calm pool

Berthing thruster

Retractable thrusters

Riser

Cameras

Well head

REFINING OIL

Most of the useful hydrocarbon molecules in crude oil are jumbled together and have to be separated out at an oil refinery. The process used to refine oil is distillation, which is based on the fact that different parts of oil boil at different temperatures. By heating the crude oil to a particular temperature, and then cooling the vapour that is given off, one particular product can be collected. Oil refineries use a continuous process in which the oil vapour rises through a column, with the various products collected at progressively higher levels. Before distillation, crude oil is treated to turn some of the thick oil into lighter, more useful oil. This process is known as cracking. Refineries use chemicals known as catalysts to speed up the cracking and make it more efficient.

▽ Oil refinery, France

DISTILLATION COLUMN

Inside the column, the oil vapour rises through holes in a series of metal trays that get progressively cooler towards the top. The lowest trays collect bitumen and the thickest oils, and only the petroleum gases reach the top.

More than 2,300 different products can be obtained from crude oil. About half of them are lubricating oils, but there are also at least 40 different types of petrol. These are then blended back together in order to produce the fuel that we put in our cars.

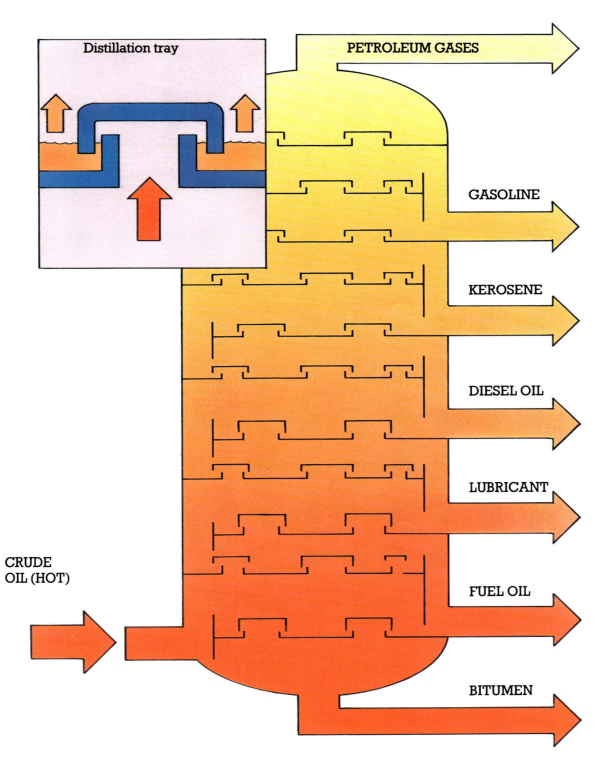

Distillation tray

PETROLEUM GASES

GASOLINE

KEROSENE

DIESEL OIL

LUBRICANT

CRUDE
OIL (HOT)

FUEL OIL

BITUMEN

REFINING GAS

Some "dry" gas can be used straight from the ground, but most natural gas has to be refined first. As well as other gases, "wet" gas may also contain a substantial amount of a number of naturally occurring petrols, which are known as "condensates".

When refining gas, the basic process is one of cooling rather than heating. After being cleaned, the gas passes through a series of compressors. These force all the hydrocarbons other than methane to condense into liquids, which can be piped off under pressure. The methane can then be cooled to below -161.5°C, at which point it too becomes a liquid. Liquid methane, also known as liquefied natural gas (LNG), is stored in underground tanks, surrounded by a layer of frozen soil many metres thick.

SEPARATION PLANT

After passing through the slug catcher, the raw gas is piped through the extraction plant, which removes the natural gas liquids from the methane. These are then piped through a series of fractionating plants that separate out the different gases. This is usually done by heating the cold liquid gas, but can be done by absorbing the gases in liquids.

The slug catcher removes water and any other "heavy" impurities with a series of mechanical and chemical filters.

Slug catcher

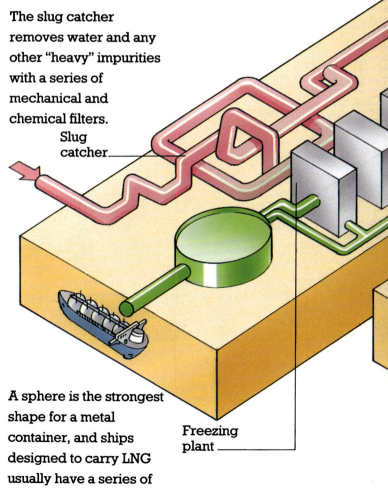

A sphere is the strongest shape for a metal container, and ships designed to carry LNG usually have a series of spherical tanks.

Freezing plant

Dry natural gas contains about 98 per cent methane, while wet gases average about 80 per cent. The next most important products are propane and butane. These are often referred to as the liquid petroleum gases (LPG), because they can be stored under pressure as liquids. The other gas, ethane, can be piped straight to the chemical industry.

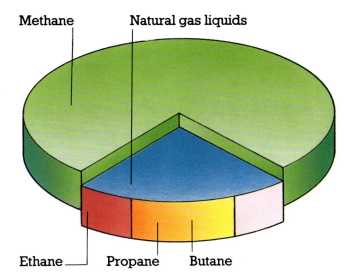

Methane   Natural gas liquids

Ethane   Propane   Butane

Extraction plant

After extraction, methane may be piped straight into a distribution system.

After fractionation, propane and butane are compressed into liquids before being stored or shipped.

Fractionating plant

Pressuring

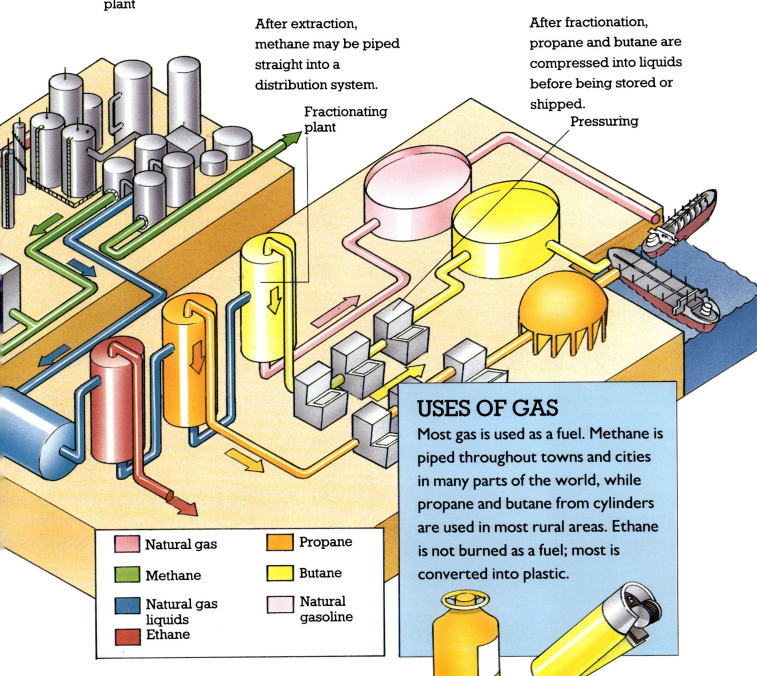

Natural gas
Methane
Natural gas liquids
Ethane
Propane
Butane
Natural gasoline

USES OF GAS

Most gas is used as a fuel. Methane is piped throughout towns and cities in many parts of the world, while propane and butane from cylinders are used in most rural areas. Ethane is not burned as a fuel; most is converted into plastic.

BURNING OIL AND GAS

A wide range of fuels is produced from oil. These are used to provide heat, electricity, and energy for transportation. Petrol, which fuels the internal combustion engine in most cars, is probably the most important and the most widely used. Diesel, which requires a different kind of engine, fuels lorries, some cars, trains and ships. Many power stations and domestic heating boilers burn fuel oil, the thickest of the liquid fuels. Paraffin is used for portable domestic heaters, and is also a major ingredient of jet aviation fuel.

Gas produces fewer fumes when it is burned than liquid fuels do, and is widely used in kitchens and for domestic heating, either from the mains (natural gas), or from pressurized metal containers (LPG).

Butane does not require much pressure to keep it liquid, and can be stored in aluminium cans (for picnic stoves) and even in plastic cigarette lighters. Propane requires greater pressure, and is distributed in heavy, armoured cylinders.

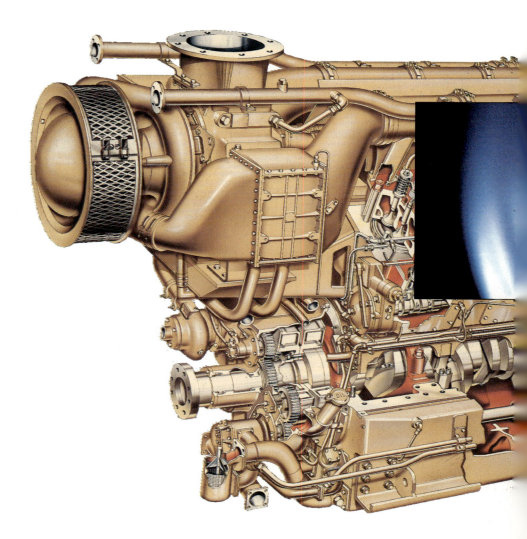

In the case of petrol, paraffin and diesel, it is not the liquid fuel that burns, but a mixture of the vapour and air. Because these fuels give off vapour even at room temperature, they must be stored and used under carefully controlled conditions. Without proper precautions, there is always a risk of explosion.

Natural gas has to be mixed with air before it will burn with a steady flame. The design of the burner on a gas appliance is extremely important because different gases require different proportions of air in order to burn safely and efficiently.

OIL AND GAS PRODUCTS

Oil and gas have given rise to a huge petrochemical industry based on useful chemicals obtained from refineries. Many hydrocarbons, of which ethane is only one, are used as raw materials in the manufacture of plastics, nylon and other artificial fibres. Some refinery products are easily converted into basic chemicals. An example is ammonia, which can be used in the manufacture of artificial fertilizer and animal feed. Hundreds of millions of tonnes of hydrocarbons are used in such ways each year. Other aspects of the petrochemical industry are concerned with much smaller quantities of very complex hydrocarbons. Many dyes, drugs and laboratory chemicals are derived from oil and gas, often using very complicated chemical processes.

Hydrocarbon molecules can form long chains known as polymers. Such polymers are the basic constituent of the wide variety of plastics available.

The petrochemical industry provides farmers with most of their insecticide and weedkiller, as well as with some fertilizer and animal feed.

Some refinery products can be used in their basic form, with little or no further chemical processing. Solvents used in dry-cleaning, carbon black in printers ink, asphalt on roads, and waxes in furniture polish are all refined from oil.

Some scientists believe that oil and gas are too valuable a source of chemicals to be wasted by burning as fuel. In the long term, they may well be correct. But in the short term, we are very much dependent on the continued use of gas and oil to supply many of our energy needs, and alternatives are not always easily available.

FOSSIL FUEL FACTS

Coal is normally measured in tonnes, gas in cubic metres, and oil in barrels (each containing 159 litres). Oil is our most important fuel, and the barrel of oil has come to represent a certain quantity of energy. The Earth's resources of fossil fuels are therefore most easily compared if they are expressed in billions of barrels of oil or their equivalent (bbrl). A billion is a thousand million – 1,000,000,000. Many scientists believe that we have so far only discovered the location of a small fraction of Earth's total fuel reserves. Estimated reserves are much greater than known and proven reserves.

Coal is the most abundant fuel, and reserves are estimated at 86,000bbrl. Of these, only 5,400bbrl are proven.

Proven oil reserves stand at about 650bbrl, with an estimated 1,100bbrl yet to be discovered, giving a total of 1,750bbrl. Proven gas reserves are nearly 400bbrl, with about 1,200bbrl still to be found, totalling about 1,600bbrl. Total world reserves of conventional oil and gas resources thus stand at 3,350 bbrl. In addition to this, there are some 6,150bbrl in tar sands and oil shales.

The use of coal as a fuel is on the decline, while oil and gas consumption is rising steadily. Nearly 75 per cent of the energy we get from fossil fuels now comes from oil and gas. At present rates of consumption, proven reserves could be exhausted within 40 years and by the year 2100 we could have used up all the world's fossil fuels.

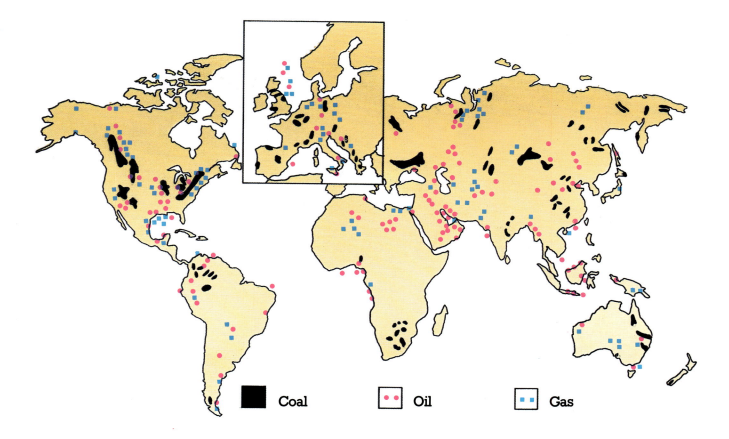

■ Coal   :•: Oil   :▪: Gas

GLOSSARY

anticline dome-shaped rock formation, often deep below the surface, where oil and gas tend to accumulate.

butane one of the two liquid petroleum gases (LPG).

catalyst any substance that assists a chemical reaction without being changed by the reaction itself. Catalysts are used at oil refineries to make distillation more efficient.

coal tar thick, black liquid that can be extracted from coal. Like crude oil, coal tar contains many different chemical substances.

condensates liquid hydrocarbons — mainly paraffins and petrols — that are found in most deposits of natural gas.

geology study of the Earth, its rocks, and their formations.

hydrocarbons chemical compounds that contain hydrogen and carbon, such as those found in crude oil.

methane natural gas; the gas that is distributed by pipe to individual homes.

overburden layer of soil and rock that is removed to expose a coal seam for open-cast mining.

plankton minute aquatic plants and animals.

propane one of the two liquid petroleum gases (LPG).

strata layers of sedimentary rock.

Useful addresses

British Coal
Hobart House
Grosvenor Place
London SW1
Tel: 071 235 2020

British Gas
Rivermill House
152 Grosvenor Road
London SW1
Tel: 071 821 1444

British Petroleum
Britannic House
Moor Lane
London
EC2Y 9BU
Tel: 071 920 8000

Department of Energy
Thames House South
Millbank
London
SW1P 4QJ
Tel: 071 238 3000

Department of the
Environment
2 Marsham Street
London SW1
Tel: 071 276 3000

INDEX